FEB

W9-AYF-695

Cuba

by Rachel Anne Cantor

Consultant: Karla Ruiz
Teachers College, Columbia University
New York, New York

BEARPORT PUBLISHING

New York, New York

Credits

Cover, © Sergey Novikov/Shutterstock and © lazyllama/Shutterstock; 3, © Alleksander/Shutterstock; 4, © Kamira/Shutterstock; 5T, © Anna Jedynak/Shutterstock; 5B, © The Visual Explorer/Shutterstock; 7, © Radius Images/Alamy; 8–9, © vicnt/iStock; 9, © Vlad61/Shutterstock; 10, © Duc Dao/Shutterstock; 11T, © Johann Helgason/Shutterstock; 11B, © krechet/Shutterstock; 12T, © Heritage Image Partnership/Alamy; 12B, © Brigida_Soriano/iStock; 13, © Tamara Kushch/Shutterstock; 14B, © Lefteris Papaulakis/123rf.com; 14–15, © Gil.K/Shutterstock; 16, © Denys Turavtsov/Shutterstock; 17, © Lya_Cattel/iStock; 18–19, © Kamira/Shutterstock; 20, © LWA/Dann Tardif Blend Images/Newscom; 21T, © Alain Lauga/Shutterstock; 21B, © Dream79/Shutterstock; 22–23, © Lisa F. Young/Shutterstock; 23T, © bonchan/Shutterstock; 23B, © GooDween123/Shutterstock; 24, © age fotostock/Alamy Stock Photo; 25, © Charles O. Cecil/Alamy Stock Photo; 26, © Kamira/Shutterstock; 27, © Marcin Krzyzak/Shutterstock; 28, © rmnoa357/Shutterstock; 29T, © Alex Staroseltsev/Shutterstock; 29B, © Chris Schneider/Associated Press; 30T, © Anton_Ivanov/Shutterstock; 30B, © Vladimir Wrangel/Shutterstock; 31 (T to B), © Kamira/Shutterstock, © Vlad61/Shutterstock, © Gil.K/Shutterstock, © vicnt/iStock, and © Johann Helgason/Shutterstock; 32, © Andrey Lobachev/Shutterstock.

Publisher: Kenn Goin
Editor: Jessica Rudolph
Creative Director: Spencer Brinker
Design: Debrah Kaiser
Photo Researcher: Olympia Shannon

Library of Congress Cataloging-in-Publication Data

Names: Cantor, Rachel Anne.
Title: Cuba / by Rachel Anne Cantor.
Description: New York, New York : Bearport Publishing, 2016.|Series: Countries We Come From| Includes
   bibliographical references and index.
Identifiers: LCCN 2015037937| ISBN 9781943553358 (library binding) | ISBN
   1943553351 (library binding)
Subjects: LCSH: Cuba—Juvenile literature.
Classification: LCC F1758.5 .C365 2016 | DDC 972.91—dc23
LC record available at http://lccn.loc.gov/2015037937

For more information, write to Bearport Publishing Company, Inc., 45 West 21st Street, Suite 3B, New York, New York 10010. Printed in the United States of America.

10 9 8 7 6 5 4 3

Contents

This Is Cuba 4

Fast Facts 30

Glossary 31

Index 32

Read More 32

Learn More Online 32

About the Author 32

This Is Cuba

Warm

Colorful

Lively

Cuba is an island country in the Caribbean Sea.

It's only 93 miles (150 km) from the United States.

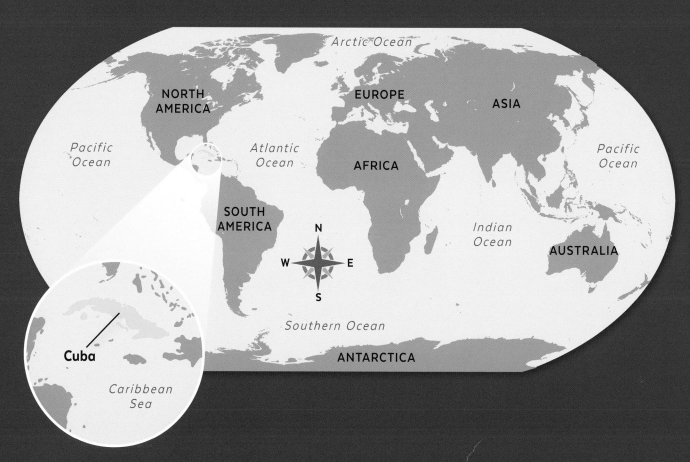

Arctic Ocean

NORTH AMERICA

EUROPE

ASIA

Pacific Ocean

Atlantic Ocean

AFRICA

Pacific Ocean

SOUTH AMERICA

N
W   E
S

Indian Ocean

AUSTRALIA

Southern Ocean

ANTARCTICA

Cuba

Caribbean Sea

Cuba is the largest country in the Caribbean.

Cuba has beautiful hills and mountains.

It also has flat **plains**.

mountains

a plain

Sunny beaches surround the island.

There are **coral reefs** in the water near the beaches.

Many interesting animals live in Cuba.

Tiny hummingbirds zip through the air.

Huge crocodiles live in **swamps**.

The hutia lives in forests and on plains. It's similar to a guinea pig. However, it's the size of a cat!

The Taíno (TYE-noh) people lived in Cuba for hundreds of years.

Spanish people took over the island in the 1500s.

stone art made by the Taíno

a church built by the Spanish

They brought slaves from Africa.

Today, many Cubans are part Taíno, part Spanish, and part African.

In the 1800s, Cubans fought for their freedom from Spain and won.

Cuban people celebrate their **independence** with parades.

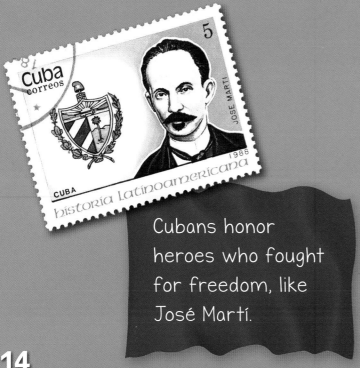

Cubans honor heroes who fought for freedom, like José Martí.

a parade in Cuba

Most Cubans speak Spanish.

In Spanish, the word for *hello* is:

Hola (OH-lah)

Some Cubans also speak African or Taíno languages. In school, many students learn English, too.

The word for *good-bye* is:

Adiós (ah-dee-YOHS)

Havana is the country's **capital**. It's also Cuba's biggest city.

More than two million people live in Havana.

Cubans have many kinds of jobs.

Some work as teachers or doctors.

Other people work on farms.

They grow plants such as sugarcane.

Sugarcane is used to make sugar.

a sugarcane farm

Cuban food is very tasty!

One popular meal includes beans, rice, meat, and fried plantains.

Plantains are similar to bananas.

plantains

Cubans often drink espresso (eh-SPREH-soh) after a meal. This is a strong type of coffee.

23

Some Cuban girls have a special party when they turn 15.

It's called a Quinceañera (*keen*-say-ah-NYEH-rah).

The birthday girl wears a beautiful dress.

Girls are driven through town on their special day. They greet family and friends.

Traditional Cuban music is called *son* (SOHN).

It has a fast beat.

Son is played with guitars and other instruments.

Some cuban musicians perform on city streets.

What's one sport
Cubans love?

Baseball!

Some of the world's biggest baseball stars are Cuban.

José Abreu is from Cuba. He plays for an American baseball team called the Chicago White Sox.

Fast Facts

Capital city: Havana

Population of Cuba: More than 11 million

Main language: Spanish

Money: Peso

Major religion: Catholic

Nearby countries include: Haiti, the Dominican Republic, Jamaica, the United States

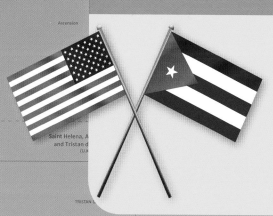

Cool Fact: For more than 50 years, Cubans and Americans weren't allowed to go to each other's countries. Recently, this law was changed. Now, Americans and Cubans can visit each other!

capital (KAP-uh-tuhl) a city where a country's government is based

coral reefs (KORE-uhl REEFS) rock-like structures formed from the skeletons of sea animals called coral polyps

independence (in-di-PEN-duhnss) freedom

plains (PLAYNZ) large, flat areas of land

swamps (SWAHMPS) low areas of land that are mostly flooded

31

Index

African people 12–13
animals 10–11
cities 18, 30
coral reefs 9
farms 21

food 21, 22–23
jobs 20–21
languages 16–17, 30
music 26–27

Quinceañera 24–25
Spanish people 12–13, 14
sports 28–29
Taíno people 12–13

Read More

Cavallo, Anna. *Cuba (Country Explorers).* Minneapolis, MN: Lerner (2011).

Wright, David K. *Cuba (Enchantment of the World).* New York: Scholastic (2009).

Learn More Online

To learn more about Cuba, visit
www.bearportpublishing.com/CountriesWeComeFrom

About the Author

Rachel Anne Cantor is a writer who lives in New Jersey.